Praise for
90 is the new

"Ginzberg's sixth poetry collection blends gratitude and grief, and reveals the poet's intact moral center and ferocity. Resilience and passion drive these poems, while wisdom delivers lines like:

> the rain and the fire
> they keep us real
> our touching
> keeps us whole

With her keen eye, generous heart, and clear mind, the poet rages not only against injustice, but the sorrow and frailty that age includes, while her *joie de vivre* insists:

> bring me the quick and easy joy
> and bring it now

This survivor's inspiring record makes clear that creative longevity is not for the lazy or faint of heart."

—GWYNN O'GARA, author of *Snake Woman Poems, Fixer-Upper, Winter at Green Haven,* and *Sea Cradles.*
Sonoma County Poet Laureate, 2010-1012

"Vilma Ginzberg's new book of poems is pure delight, though not all of the subjects are delightful. It's the poet's language that brings light to every corner of her life and illuminates the world in which she lives, which is also in large part our world. A reader can begin anywhere: at the start, in the middle, or even at the end with the poem that's titled 'reflections on the New Year's Eve of my 91st' in which Ginzberg takes stock of her life today and offers wisdom to those younger than her in years. For those who have listened to Ginzberg read aloud, these poems ought to bring a double delight; one can't help but hear the sound of her voice as you follow the words on the page. Ginzberg has been publishing her poetry in Sonoma County for 14 years. '90 is the new,' her latest book, shows that she has not lost her passion, compassion and sense of humor. Open this volume and celebrate with a poet who has kept her language young and alive through fires and ashes, grief and glory."

—JONAH RASKIN, author of *Rock 'n' Roll Women*

"As always, Vilma puts into words that which is otherwise subliminal. Her clarity and good humor invite my own unrealized thoughts or musings to emerge, and I find myself nodding, smiling and appreciating the gift of deeper intimacy with myself."

—ANNELISA MACBEAN, PhD

90 is the new

Also by Vilma Olsvary Ginzberg

Poems

Colors of Glass, iUniverse, 2004

Present at the Creation, Ed. with Doug Stout, Small Poetry Press, 2006

Murmurs & Outcries, Small Poetry Press, 2007

Snake Pit, Round Barn Press, 2010

I Don't Know How to Do This, poems on aging, Meridien Pressworks, 2011

making noise, McCaa Books, 2013

Memoir

When the Iris Blooms, 2012

Mostly Roses, 2015

In Process

Out of Context, poems from my eighties, 2018

Octogenarian on Fire, memoir, 2018

90 is the new

Poems

Vilma Olsvary Ginzberg

McCaa Books • Santa Rosa

McCaa Books
1604 Deer Run
Santa Rosa, CA 95405

Copyright © 2018 by Vilma Olsvary Ginzberg
All Rights Reserved

Without limiting the rights under copyright reserved above, no part of this publication may be reproduced, distributed, or transmitted in any form or by any means, or stored in a database or retrieval system, without the prior written permission of both the copyright owner and the publisher of this book except in the case of brief quotations embodied in critical articles or reviews.

Library of Congress Control Number: 2018953213

ISBN 978-0-9996956-5-4

First published in 2018 by McCaa Books,
an imprint of McCaa Publications.

Printed in the United States of America
Set in Tahoma

Author's photo by Christine Caliandro.
Cover photos by Geri Cross.

www.mccaabooks.com

For R-P,
who eschews hyperbole
but loves these poems

Contents

pregnancy   11

nature

for all things there is a season   15
eclipse 2017   16

the fires

firestorm   18
refugees   19
waiting it out   20
after-fire language   21
the grief of ashes the ashes of grief   22

out there

hand on the Bible   25
dear Charleston   26
for MIke Tuggle   27
April 15   28
baby sister at 85   29
she appears to have passed   30

in here

balancing act   35
three deaths   36
energy deficit   38
undependence   41
side effect   42
reflections on the eve of my 91st   43

About the Author   45

pregnancy

it waits there
this unborn poem
its eyes unformed
its own flame as yet unsparked
its hands mere buds
unable to yet hold its thought
its shape not of itself's becoming

I cradle it
with my enveloping darkness
protect it
from the blinding light
of even my own
inquiry

it will come
in its time
I say to no one
but itself

and if not
I already know
how to mourn
the unborn
with a respectful silence
and gratitude
all too familiar

nature

for all things there is a season

Hold off, my August-blooming children!
May is not your time.
What will be left for you to do
in what should be your prime?

Patience be your marching step,
trust your holding rein.
When the summer sun invites,
you will bloom again.

Keep your blossoms hid for now.
Wait to sing your song.
Life is short, the seasons set.
It will all move along.

Stretch your passion, make it last
for yet another while;
Waiting for the rip'ning blush
will grant us all a smile.

Be not rash to rush the clock.
Stroll the weeks away.
Breathe the scents, bathe in the breeze.
Nothing's here to stay.

Eclipse 2017

we watch this cosmic pair
in their rare dance

great fiery mass
father of all life
ruling all in its orbit
defining day and night
on this blue ball of rock and sea
we call home

and this weaker orb of measured visit
mirror of the great sun's light
whose feeble glow bounces off his radiance
while waxing and waning her monthly way
in and out of our night-dreams

on this 21st day of this august month
marching her fullness out
in broad daylight
she becomes the dark presence
who blocks his power
who shrinks his fire to a mere perimeter
daring the arrogant
to dismiss her

anomaly of nature
womb of superstition
specter of fear to our uninformed forebears
this mid-day darkness
this dance of light and dark
swaths its way across the continent
bringing together
the naïve and the knowledgeable
the innocent and the instructed
all one in solemn awe
on this uncertainly spinning globe

the fires
Santa Rosa CA, October 2017

Vilma's reading of these five fire poems was used in a PBS documentary made by KRCB-TV for an anniversary retrospective on the 2017 fires, aired on October 8, 2018.

firestorm

east wind bodes ill
turning fierce
whipping any loose thing
into weapon

the afternoon sky grows dark

awakened at 3 a.m. into blackened room
power out
the only light the sky
glowering red
above the rooftops

floating flashlights appear
dance briefly
then leave
questions in their wake

east wind brings trouble
fierce reckless fiery trouble
fast furious unstoppable trouble
wind and fire
flowing like lava
over the hills into the valleys
through the innocent sleeping neighborhoods
undiscerning   unpredictable
flaming monster devouring the landscape

refugees

For Puerto Rico, Mexico City, Houston, Florida, Northern California, Africa, and all refugees everywhere

ripped from daily habit
torn from the arms of familiar
stripped of everything but the nakedness of now

we are refugees

disaster triggers adrenalin
adrenalin triggers response
we respond with amazing acuity
energy sufficient
generosity beyond resource
resourcefulness beyond supply
always, creativity
    peppered with wit

we are refugees

our common circumstance makes us tribal
    intimate
    gentle or ferocious, as needed
old barriers vanish
private shadows disappear
    in the light of need
we make do
    accept gifts
    celebrate the thinnest of choice
discover talent
    ours and others'
inconvenience melts away under gratitude

we are refugees

discovering our real home
    in the broken mending heart
        of community

waiting it out

morning

white banana moon

smiles at

still leaves

silent birds hide

is it respite

or

warning

after-fire language

are you ok? is the question

the lucky ones tell tales of inconvenience
even adventure

but sometimes the answer is simply
I'm still here or we're still here
and we know the unspeakable has happened

it's in the voice
and the slight bend of neck
a certain emptiness of eye
the paucity of words
those who lost everything have lost their tongue
as have we

I'm sorry we stutter
for your loss is what we think
with some unspoken survivor guilt creeping in behind

and thank goodness we say in our helpless little tones
weakly affirming the big gift so often taken for granted

what else is there to say
that is neither Pollyanna nor intrusive
we offer hugs to strangers as well as the beloved
write bigger checks
drop clothes into receiving bins
wonder what else we can do

fire: the great and fearsome leveler
has once more made family of us all
as we fall into the after-fire language
of gratitude and grief
that exhausting silent companion-pair
of the new normal

the grief of ashes the ashes of grief
For Kathyrn Kubota

she comes here every day
sits in her car
before her the now razed lot
she once for so many decades called home
and cries

for the lost photo albums
the jewelry marking special love occasions
the marriage license
the birth certificates
the transfer deeds
the saved greeting cards
the grandchildren's drawings on the fridge and the china and
the silver and the carved wood and the stainless steel and the
linens and the silk ties and the cotton comforters and the
leather belts and the shoes in the closets and under the beds
and the jackets for all seasons and the books including the
open one on her nightstand and the tools in the garage and in
her kitchen drawers and the last embroideries of her grand-
mother's arthritic knuckles
and every time she remembers another lost thing

and she cries dry tears
she is so empty anymore

no pierced and dented cup of hope
can hold a single watery word of comfort

all is gone

all that is left is her grief
held like a stone heart in the pit of her being
ashen as the anonymous debris
she once called home

I feel as if I have been erased
she says

out there

hand on the Bible

he puts his hand
the one he bragged
could grab any woman's crotch
because he is
a star

he puts that hand
on the same Bible
Lincoln's work-roughened hand
graced

the same Bible
Obama's generous palm
gently laid on

he puts that vile hand
on that sacred Bible

and I am coiled to my core
by nausea

Dear Charleston, and Columbine, and Baton Rouge, and Sandy Hook, and Dallas, and Charlottesville, and ……… the names are too many to remember ……

just a note to let you know
I'm thinking of you

with apology

that I don't have arms enough
to embrace your sorrow

tears enough for the ocean of sadness

love enough
to fill the canyons
left gaping in your world

fire enough to melt the avalanche of hatred
waiting every day

words enough for

the

impossible

ineffable

outrage

for Mike Tuggle
Poet, fellow laureate 2008/2009

Author of *The Singing Itself* and *Absolute Elsewhere*

and the days months years crawled by
leaving an unexpected week
on my wall

where were you all this time?

here is your name
fading on my to-do list

I meant to call

suddenly you are gone

and the Cazadero redwoods whisper your name
to the nighthawks
and the weeping moon

and dim do I hear you
strong-legged and Okie-drawled
singing
to the absolute elsewhere

April 15

I emerge
from the deep sea
of churning numbers
dripping sums
and subtrahends
gasping for a breath
of digit-free air

baby sister at 85

the fog of forgetting
that once cooled
the frantic fires of busy-ness
has slowly crept closer
the haze closing in
blurring out first the faraway
beyond the reach of time
and place

now the daze creeps slowly nearer
blotting out the face of neighbors
birthdays of the beloved
threatening to steal
names from those dearest
permanently linked progeny
the very ties of blood

what remains is the never-ending now
that within reach of hand and eye and ear
this chair of lumps and comforts
this wallpaper newly-discovered
this bird singing one-on-one
this plate of sweets
all too soon gone from memory

while time disappears
like sand
through the fingers of her days
she hangs on
for dear life
to this nano-second
weaving shreds of fantasy and fear
into scattered scraps of meaning

she appears to have passed peacefully in her sleep   For Joan

is she a she
can we still call her that
a she is one who lives, responds, acts
as she did just yesterday
whatever is left in her silent bed
can we still call by that word she
she

appears
appears is all we can say
for we do not know
no one of us was there to witness
we can only surmise
by her appearance
she appears

to have passed
what a heavy phrase
to have passed
it is a mighty passage
a profound change
a thunderous turn
that rocks the worlds
of so many
to say nothing of the she
who made the passage
and we have so many questions
unknowingly we ask
unwillingly we wonder
how it was
to have passed

to have passed peacefully
peacefully
as if that is the preferred way

so contrary to the urge
to rage rage against the dying
the dying of the light
to come to terms
with that so final a change
that must be the last fervent hope
of the unwilling
to pass peacefully

peacefully
in her sleep
or at least we surmise
it was in her sleep
or some other quiet state
for we cannot imagine
passing peacefully while awake
we would rather
imagine being rocked
by motherly arms into peaceful slumber
that last sleep
that long final last big sleep
from which there is no waking
to this particular day
when

she was found

appearing

to have passed

peacefully

in her sleep

may it be so

in here

balancing act

the world is always on trial these days
living in this old body
tests my endurance daily
every planned endeavor
accompanied by
the silent secret companion dare:
this better be worth it

too often it isn't

yet the joys abide
short as they are
in the ocean of challenges:
hot soup
watching the spider spin her web
scribing whatever poem appears
talking with you on the phone
Mozart from the radio
dark chocolate
petting a dog any dog
getting home and sitting down
my head on the pillow
dreaming, most of the time

so pardon me if I say no
it is not personal
it is this body older than I
making my life more tentative

what did I do to deserve this
I ask the empty room
the only answer I hear
is the cruel voice of time

nothing personal it says

three deaths

since I was born into this name
three deaths have I already died

at the start
sturdy and eager
was I to be reunited
with this planet I adored
but died before I even saw light
with my head stuck in the crook
of my mother's hip bone
panicked pained then lifeless
I was dragged out
by the cold steel hands of medicine
my innate will and inherited strength
insisting me into
the life I so desired

I died a second time at 12
innocently sucked by the dark undertow
of the seductive atlantic
into deep black sleep of no return
placid pale then lifeless
I was dragged out
by unknown rescue of man or the sea itself
I'll never know
onto cold wet beach
where sand and salty sea were pushed
out of my lungs
burning stinging scraping
up through my child-tender throat
making room once again
for the clear cloudless air
that I might stay
somewhat longer
on this kind blue earth

once again did I die

a diminished and wrinkled 89
after poeming for peace and justice
with my beloved confreres
this time drowning
not in the expanse of endless ocean
but in the confines
of my own claustrophobic lungs
filling with forbidden liquid
drowning in my own
misdirected fluids

an unnamed merciful fate
gifted me a stranger
rescuer healer who hurried me
to harried hospital halls of help
where
after days
I was awakened
like some fabled sleeping princess
by the cold plastic metal kiss
of an impersonal ventilator
adding daylight savings hours
to my waning years

hoarding gratitude like a homeless pilgrim
I know but this:
that empty blackness waits
waits still
where the sundial casts no shadow

meanwhile
questions whisper to the night
if life is a schoolroom
what am I to learn?
if life is a treasure hunt
what is the coveted prize?
if life is a cabaret
what song am I to sing?

energy deficit

I don't have much energy left
to try to change the world
though heaven knows
it needs improving

but after groaning myself
out of bed a-mornings
and taking my vitals
a daily chore ever since that heart thing

and with the slowness of the tortoise
getting dressed
and all that goes before and after

and making breakfast
[scrambling the eggs seems like a workout anymore]
and keeping track of the vitamins
for my doc and for me

and reading the morning paper
and meditating that away

and cleaning up the kitchen

and making the bed
oh making the bed
that ought to be the new workout
instead of the gym

and putting away the laundered clothes
washed yesterday

and checking my email
to see if the family is still OK
and seeing that the family of nations
is not

and weather permitting
checking to see how my garden is faring
what with the drought
and poor air and all
and musing how
the weeds and snails shall overcome some day
but meanwhile trying to hold my own
in their midst

and picking the ripening fruit
and putting it out
on the communal table
feeling a bit of eden in my bones

and coming back in
stomping off the dirt
washing my hands
and sitting for a minute
to rest the weary back

and then to the desk
to track my budget
and pay my bills
and make a list
for the next foray of chores

and making the appointments
for the teeth
and the heart
and the knees
and the trainer
and the hair
and the taxes
and the toenail trim

and calling my sister
now failing to remember
and crying after hanging up

and texting my granddaughter
that I'll love her always

and quick
write down that phrase
so it's not lost
because the poetry isn't coming
as often as it used to

and noticing how much of the day
has been used up

and there's so much still to do
another meal or two
a call or two to friends
not counting the guilty pleasure tv show
and getting ready for bed
in this little world
I call my life
at something past ninety

no wonder
I don't have much energy left
to try to change the world
though heaven knows
it needs improving

undependence

solidly at home
these many decades
with my fierce self-reliance
a familiar and well-practiced
habit of self-view

I am not accustomed
to asking for aid
nor indeed comfortable
when it is offered unbidden

on the contrary
I am like a criminal witnessed
in the vulnerability
I have tried so hard to hide
now revealed by your offer
and announced to the world
and worse still to me

your gift I know is kind
feels accusatory
a betrayal, an outing

since I have no practice
in gracious acceptance
I must ask your pardon
for my clumsy or grumpy reply
or worse, disregard

in trying to cut away from my weakness
I cut away instead
from you

if that succeeds I am alone
with my despised new companion
frailty

side effect: a sad poem for Grandparents Day

where once we used to spend
our time together
catching up on family
marveling at
the myriad wonders
of nature
the dazzling minutae
of the universe
the mysteries of life and death

today I fill
our hour
with the array
of medicine bottles
and side effects
show off
the new cane
easier for me to use
gather my wrap
around my chilled shoulders
like I used to
gather your words
to warm my soul

swathed in embarrassment
I hug you goodbye
the nagging feeling
hovering
that it will be a while
before you come back

reflections on the New Year's Eve of my 91st

the days are growing shorter
and the time ahead shrinks
as do I

I have no longer patience
for unraveling the unrevealed
as this abode crumbles to its destiny

I have no time anymore
for the obtuse

I prefer the compact
to the complex
the haiku to the epic
the song to the symphony
the rose to the garden

there is sorrow large enough
looming ahead

bring me the quick and easy joy
and bring it now

your newest poem
the forbidden treat
a lingering hug

tell me your truth
and dare hear mine
but wallow shall we not

the rain and the fire
they keep us real
our touching
keeps us whole

about the author

In her nineties, Vilma continues to write, to mentor younger poets, and to host and attend poetry reading venues. vilmaginz@aol.com.

www.ingramcontent.com/pod-product-compliance
Lightning Source LLC
Chambersburg PA
CBHW070750050426
42449CB00010B/2402